Earth, Sun and Moon

By the end of this book you will know more about:

- The shape and size of the Earth, Sun and Moon.
- How the Earth, Sun and Moon move.

You will:

- Use books, the Internet and CD-ROMs to help you answer questions.
- Do a survey.
- Draw a graph.

Task
1

What do you know about the Earth, Sun and Moon?

Maybe you think that:

- The Earth is a planet. It is made of rock, air and water.

- The Sun is a star. It gives us heat and light.

- The Moon is made of rock. Nothing lives on the Moon.

Earth and Moon

The Sun

Maybe you think that:

- The Earth is flat.

- The Sun is the same size as the Moon.

- The Moon is made of cheese.

⚐ Discuss all your ideas with the class.

⚐ How could you find out if your ideas are correct?

The Moon

There are some things about the Earth, Sun and Moon that you cannot prove for yourself. You have to look at what other people have found out. You have to decide whether their evidence is good enough.

By the end of this book you will know that the Earth, Sun and Moon are spheres; that they are very different in size; and that they are moving.

The Earth, Sun and Moon are spheres.
Sometimes you cannot test things directly, but
you can learn from what others have found out.

Task 2 — It's a round world

1

It is 2200 years ago. You are standing close to a deep well in the Egyptian city of Syene. Next to you is Eratosthenes, a Greek scientist. It is midday and the Sun is at its highest in the sky.

"Look!" says Eratosthenes, and you both peer down the well. "The light is shining to the very bottom, this happens at midday on this same day every year. Now, if the Earth is flat, the Sun should be shining to the bottom of every well in the world at this moment!"

"And is it?"

"Certainly not. I've been in Alexandria, to the north of here on this same day and I know the Sun isn't lighting up the wells there at all at midday. In fact, it is casting shadows, because it isn't overhead."

"Why is that?"

"It's obvious!" says Eratosthenes. "It's because the world is round!"

✪ Some people still think that the Earth is flat. How would you convince them that the Earth is a sphere, the shape of a ball? Draw and write to show your ideas.

✪ Use Task Sheet 1 to help you.

Eratosthenes was right

There are other ways of showing that the Earth is round:

- You can travel round the world.

- When ships appear over the horizon, they come over a curve. You see their masts or funnels first, then the hull.

- When there is an eclipse of the Moon, the curved shadow of the Earth is cast on the Moon's face.

- The Earth is a planet. We can see that other planets in space are not flat.

- Photographs from artificial **satellites** show that the Earth has a curved horizon and that it is a sphere.

How big?

Eratosthenes hired a man to pace out the distance from Syene to Alexandria. He found that the two places were 800 km apart. From this measurement, Eratosthenes calculated that it was about 40 000 km round the Earth.

Total solar eclipse

The Sun is much bigger than the Moon, but it is much further away from the Earth. In the sky, they appear to be the same size.

In the same way that you can 'cover' a distant mountain with your thumbnail, so the Moon occasionally covers the Sun, blotting it out completely. This is a total eclipse of the Sun.

On Wednesday, 11th August 1999, a total eclipse of the Sun was visible from much of Cornwall; parts of Devon; the Scilly Isles; and Alderney, one of the Channel Islands. At 11:11 a.m., the Moon, looking like a black disc, fitted exactly over the Sun and the sky was as dark as a moonlit night.

Task 3

Just how much bigger?

 You are going to choose three spheres that are about the right size to represent the Earth, the Sun and the Moon. The Fact File will help you.

- Choose one sphere to represent the Sun. What do you know about the Sun? Which sphere is the best choice?

- You know that the Earth is smaller than the Sun. But how much smaller? Choose a sphere to represent the Earth.

- Is the Moon smaller than the Earth? How much smaller? Choose a sphere to represent the Moon.

 Explain the reasons for your choices.

you need:

A selection of spheres, of very different sizes, such as:

- beach ball
- football
- water melon
- tennis ball
- table-tennis ball
- orange
- marble
- pea
- round bead
- peppercorns or round seeds (coriander, mustard, poppy)

Solar eclipse

The Moon

The Earth

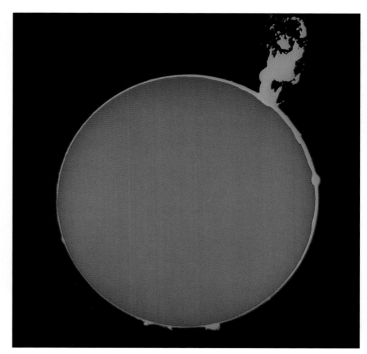

The Sun

Fact File Sun, Earth and Moon

	Circumference	**Diameter**
Sun	4 370 880 km	1 392 000 km
Earth	40 076 km	12 756 km
Moon	10 915 km	3 476 km

⭐ **The Sun appears to move across the sky through the day. You can sometimes discover different things from the same evidence.**

Copernicus and Galileo

Nicolas Copernicus

Once people believed that the Sun moved round the Earth. This is why:

- The Sun – and all the stars – seemed to move across the sky.
- The Earth felt as if it was standing still. If the Earth had been moving, people would have fallen off!
- The Earth was a very important place because that's where people lived. It made sense that everything, including the Sun, would move around it!

However, in 1543, Nicolas Copernicus, a Polish astronomer, showed that the Earth, and all the planets, including Jupiter, circled the Sun. Nobody believed his ideas. Then in 1609, Galileo Galilei, an Italian, found more evidence using a telescope to support the ideas of Copernicus. Galileo said:

- The planets, including the Earth, orbit the Sun.
- The Earth spins on its axis – an imaginary line through the centre of the Earth – once every day.

- The spin of the Earth makes the Sun appear to move in the sky.
- The Earth's atmosphere – the air around it – spins with the Earth.

Galileo used models to explain his ideas.

Galileo Galilei

The sunniest room

Which is the sunniest classroom in your school? You can find out in different ways:

1 If you know your school well, you may remember one room or area which gets very sunny, especially on hot days.

2 You could visit each room in the school and make a record of how sunny it is. You could ask children who work there whether it is it sunny in the morning, or the afternoon. Go back five or six times during the day, and see which time of day is the sunniest.

3 You could use a light or temperature sensor and a computer to make a record of the changes in each room during the day.

✨ Which room is sunny early in the morning? Which is sunny in the afternoon? Use Task Sheet 2 or a computer to display your results.

✨ Using your evidence and what you know about the Sun and the Earth from the Fact File, which of these is true?

● The Sun moves across the sky, making different classrooms sunny in the morning and in the afternoon.

● The Earth turns so that the Sun appears to move across the sky, making different classrooms sunny in the morning and in the afternoon.

Using a light sensor

What have you proved?

Many people did not believe the ideas of Galileo and Copernicus, because they would only believe the evidence of their own eyes. They saw the Sun rise – climb into the sky – sink – set and dip below the horizon. They believed they saw a moving Sun.

But the Sun does not move around the Earth – it is the Earth that moves around the Sun. To us on the moving Earth, it looks exactly as if the Sun is moving. No wonder people were confused!

The Earth spins as it moves round the Sun

Extra Challenge

 Find out more about Copernicus and Galileo using CD-ROMs and the Internet.

 **High speed**

The Earth not only moves round the Sun but it also spins or rotates at the same time. It travels round the Sun at over 100 000 km an hour and spins on its **axis** at more than 1600 km an hour. But we do not sense this movement. To us, the Earth feels as though it is standing still.

Hazel on the train

Hazel was sitting in the train with her mother. She looked out of the window on her left. She could see into another train.

She looked out of the window on her right. She could see people standing on the platform.

She looked back to her left. The windows of the train next to her were moving slowly past.

"That train is leaving the station!" she said to her mother.

"No, dear," said her mother. "That train is standing still. We are leaving the station!"

Hazel looked to her right. Sure enough, they were passing the people on the platform. Her train was moving.

✸ Put three pencils side by side on the table. The middle pencil is Hazel's train. One pencil is the other train, and one is the station.

✸ Slide the other train along. From where Hazel is sitting, she can see the train move. Return the pencil to its original position.

✸ Slide the middle pencil along. What can Hazel see from this moving train? To her, it looks just the same. It looks as if the other train is leaving the station.

Hazel's train is like the Earth, and the other train is like the Sun. Hazel's train is moving, and the other train is standing still.

The Earth spins 360° on its axis every 24 hours.

Task **6**

Street scene

The spin of the Earth gives us day and night. The part of the Earth facing the Sun is in daylight; the part facing away from the Sun is in darkness.

✦ Look at these two pictures, They show the same place. One is a daytime picture and other is at night. Look for the differences. Notice that in one picture you can see the Sun, which is a huge light source.

✦ Complete Task Sheet 3.

Fact File The biggest light source

The Sun is a gigantic light source. Its temperature is over 5000°C at the surface. In the centre the temperature is 15 000 000°C.

Although the Sun is around 150 million kilometres away, its light can still harm your eyes if you look straight at it.

Light from the Sun is reflected by the rocky surface of the Moon, which makes the Moon shine at night and gives us 'moonlight'. This is why we can see the Moon.

Sunset

Spinning Earth

☆ Work with a partner. Switch on the torch. The Sun is shining!

☆ Hold the globe or ball in front of the torch. Turn the globe slowly. The Earth turns anticlockwise.

☆ Notice how one side of the Earth is in daylight, while it is night on the other side.

☆ Now stick a tiny piece of Blu-tack on the surface of the Earth, roughly where you live. This is you – if you were taller than a mountain!

☆ Turn the Earth slowly again. What happens to 'you'?

☆ Notice that it is the Earth that is moving, not the Sun.

you need:

- strong torch (the Sun)

- globe or large ball (the Earth)

- tiny piece of Blu-tack – you!

- space in a shady place

Seeing the light

3000 years ago, maps of the world showed the Mediterranean Sea in the middle of a flat Earth. People believed that if you sailed far out into the ocean, you would fall off the edge.

✦ Give three reasons why these ideas are wrong.

You see some younger children in the playground with a shadow stick. They have marked the shadow of the stick every hour. "Look how the Sun has moved today!" they tell you.

✦ What can you tell them about their results?

✦ Read the Fact File on page 12 and study the picture opposite.
Explain why a person on Earth can see the Moon?
Where is the Sun in this picture?
Draw your ideas on Task Sheet 3, use arrows to show how the light from the Sun reflects off the Moon.

The Sun rises in the east and sets in the west. Observe the pattern in the Sun rising and setting. Represent observations on a graph.

Task 8 — Turning Earth

Don't look straight at bright lights.

- Work in groups of 5 or 6.

  Stand in a circle, all facing outward with arms linked. You are the Earth.

- The bright light – the Sun – should be facing one of you.

- Move slowly round, anticlockwise. One of you says 'Stop' at any time.

- Who is in daylight?
  Who is in darkness?
  Do this several times.

- Now move round again.

  Each of you should call out when you reach 'sunrise', 'midday', 'sunset' and 'midnight'.

- What do you notice?

you need:
- bright light
- space in a dark room

Words to learn and use:
axis
eclipse
horizon
satellite
solar
telescope

Task 9 — Back-to-back spin

you need:
- safety pins or sticky tape
- bright light
- space in a dark room
- card for labels

- Work in groups of 5 or 6.
  Make labels like this for each member of your group:

  west east

- Set up a bright light – the Sun – in a dark room.

- Each put a label on the front on your chest.

- Stand in a circle as in Task 6.

- Turn anticlockwise.

- As the Earth spins you can see how the Sun appears to rise – as you begin to see the light, and then set – as the light disappears. Notice which direction the Sun is in as it rises and sets.

- What does this tell you about sunrise and sunset?

Fact File

Daylight times

A

B

Daylight times change in the summer and winter. In the summer, the Sun shines early in the morning and daylight hours are long, and you can play outside in the light until quite late. You may even go to bed while it is still light outside.

In the winter, daylight time is shorter. The mornings are dark and you need artificial light to be able to see outdoors in the evening.

The Earth is tilted as it **orbits** the Sun, so the path the Sun appears to take across the sky, changes. In the summer, the Sun appears in the sky for longer, and climbs higher (A). In the winter, the Sun appears in the sky for a shorter time, and does not climb so high (B).

Changing daylight hours

4,5,6

The changes in daylight time follow a pattern. It is possible to predict this pattern accurately – to the minute.

These are the sunrise and sunset times for London in June, 2000.

The sunrise time is the time that the Sun rises. So on June 8th, 2000, the Sun rose at 04:45 a.m. – a quarter to five in the morning.

The sunset time is the time the Sun sets. So on June 8th, 2000, the Sun set at 21:14 – that's 9:14 p.m. (nearly a quarter past nine at night).

Sunrise and sunset times in London, June 2000

Date	Sunrise	Sunset
1	04:49	21:08
2	04:48	21:09
3	04:48	21:10
4	04:47	21:11
5	04:46	21:12
6	04:46	21:13
7	04:45	21:14
8	04:45	21:14
9	04:44	21:15
10	04:44	21:16
11	04:43	21:17
12	04:43	21:17
13	04:43	21:18
14	04:43	21:19
15	04:43	21:19
16	04:43	21:20
17	04:42	21:20
18	04:42	21:20
19	04:43	21:21
20	04:43	21:21
21	04:43	21:21
22	04:43	21:21
23	04:43	21:22
24	04:44	21:22
25	04:44	21:22
26	04:44	21:22
27	04:45	21:22
28	04:45	21:21
29	04:46	21:20
30	04:47	21:20

Use Task Sheets 4 and 5 to help you draw a graph of sunrise and sunset times for some of the days in June.

Extra Challenge

- Using the Internet, find the sunrise and sunset times for:
  - Belfast
  - Birmingham
  - Bristol
  - Glasgow
  - London
  - Manchester
  - Newcastle
- Which city is the nearest to you? Calculate how much daylight there will be on your birthday in that city.
- Record the data for you and for your friends.
  - Who has the most daylight on their birthday?
  - Who has the least?
  - What pattern can you see in the data? Use Task Sheet 6 to help you.

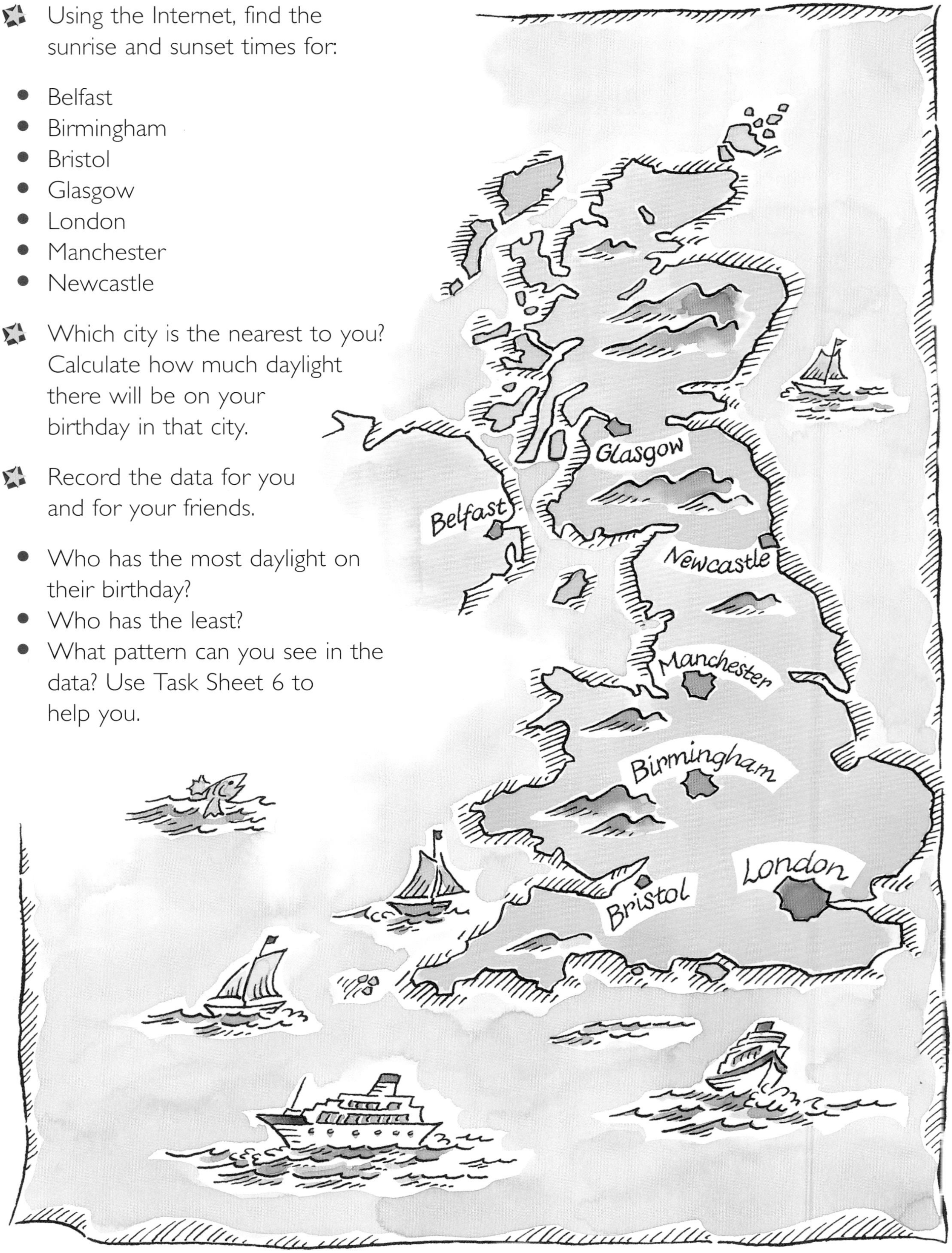

The Earth takes a year to orbit the Sun.

Modelling the Earth's orbit

✷ Work with a partner. Stand still in a space. You are the Sun.

✷ On the floor, your partner marks a position some way from the Sun. They are the Earth, and they are orbiting you. They walk round you in a big circle anticlockwise, slowly. When they get back to where they started, a year has passed.

✷ As well as orbiting, the Earth needs to rotate. They orbit again, spinning slowly anticlockwise at the same time.

✷ Remember that the Sun spins too – and it travels through space, taking the Earth with it!

One orbit is one year

Six thousand years ago, the ancient Egyptians noticed that there was a regular pattern to the stars. This pattern repeated itself every 365 days and they called this period a **year**. They divided their year into 12 months, each containing 30 days, but there were 5 days left over. They decided that on these five days they would have a great party. The party always started on the same day that Sirius the Dog Star rose in line with the Sun and the River Nile flooded to make the land fertile.

We now know that what the ancient Egyptians called a year is the same amount of time that the Earth takes to go all the way round the Sun – to make one complete orbit. But these days we no longer have to follow the pattern of the stars and Sun to know when a year has gone by – we use calendars.

✶ Explore some of the many web sites or CD-ROMs that show you how the Earth moves. You could investigate the other planets in the solar system and study their positions and movements.

The nine planets of the solar system

A birthday every four years

The Earth takes 365 ¼ days to orbit the Sun completely. This means that every four years there are four quarter days extra. We add the four quarters together and give that year – the leap year – an extra day. We add that day onto February, because it is the shortest month. In a leap year, February has 29 days.

Some people are born on February 29th, so they only have a birthday once every four years! They often celebrate their birthday on February 28th instead.

Words to learn and use:
east
moonlight
orbit
planet
rotation
solar system
west
year

⭐ **The Moon takes about 28 days to orbit the Earth. The Moon looks different during the course of a month because of its orbit.**

Task 12 Facing the Earth

Why does the Moon seem to change shape?

The Earth casts its shadow on the Moon.

Clouds cover part of the Moon.

The shadow of the Sun falls on the Moon.

you need:
- chair
- bright window

Although it orbits the Earth, the same side of the Moon always faces us. How can this happen?

✪ Work with a partner. Sit in the chair near a window with space all around you. You are the Earth.

✪ Your partner orbits the Earth by circling the chair. They are the Moon. The Moon must face the Earth all the time. The Earth always sees the same side of the Moon. How can you do this?

✪ Change places with your partner and repeat the activity two or three times.

✪ Imagine that you could watch yourselves from above. Draw a diagram to show what happens. You could use a computer.

✪ Repeat the activity. Look carefully at the light from the window. It is like the light from the Sun.

✪ When is the light on the Moon's face?

✪ When is the Moon's face in shadow?

✪ Does the Moon appear to change shape? Why?

Extra Challenge

✪ Make the model in the picture.

✪ Paint the inside of the box and lid black and let them dry.

✪ Carefully cut or punch holes along the side as shown.
Cut a hole for the torch to fit in.

✪ Hang the ball in the box using wire or a thin stick.

✪ Switch on the torch and look through each peep-hole in turn.

✪ Imagine you are the Earth, the ball is the Moon and the torch is the Sun.
Describe what the Moon looks like through each peep-hole.

✪ Notice that the Moon stays still in this model, while you – the Earth – move.
Is this what really happens?

you need:

• shoe box

• polystyrene ball or table-tennis ball

• wire or thin stick

• scissors or hole punch

• black paint and brush

• torch

⚠ *Let your teacher cut or punch holes in tough cardboard*

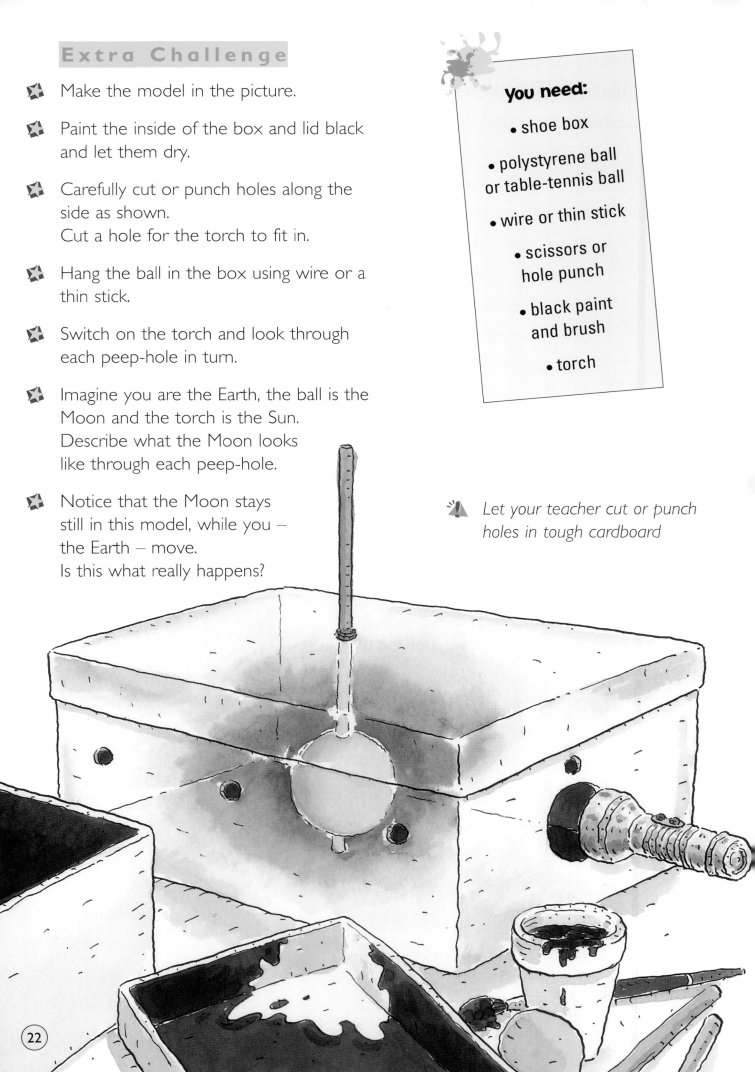

Checkpoint 2

Space explorers

✦ You are the Captain of a spaceship. You are about to fly to the Moon. But you have a problem. Your crew has some very strange ideas.

> The Moon is flat, Captain. We shall bounce off!

> It will be just as close to fly to the Sun as the Moon. They're both the same size!

> The Moon is made of cheese, Captain. And what if the little green men get us?

> We shall miss the Moon for sure. Look at it, Captain. It's tiny!

> We can't fly to the Moon tonight, Captain. Half of it is missing!

✦ Explain to the crew why they are wrong.

✦ You are on holiday in space. Design a postcard showing the most interesting facts you have learned about the Earth, Sun and Moon. You could even design a space holiday web site.

23

Summary

Which of these do you know and which can you do?

- I know that you can learn from what others have found out when you cannot test something directly.

- I know that the Earth, Sun and Moon are spheres that are very different in size.

- I know that the Sun appears to move across the sky through the day.

- I know that you can sometimes discover different things from the same evidence.

- I know that the Earth spins 360° on its axis every 24 hours.

- I know that the Sun rises in the east and sets in the west.

- I know that the Earth takes a year to orbit the Sun.

- I know that the Moon takes about 28 days to orbit the Earth.

- I know that the Moon looks different during the course of a month because of its orbit.

- I can represent my observations on a graph.

Complete your **Science Log** to show how well you know these and how well you can do them. Circle a face for each statement.